The Essential Thucydides

On Justice, Power, and Human Nature

SECOND EDITION, EXPANDED AND REVISED

Selections from
The History of the Peloponnesian War